MW00748557

Ranchin', Ropin' an' Doctorin'

A book of cowboy and veterinary cartoons

By Robert M. Miller, DVM

ISBN 978-0-9844620-3-2

Published by

Robert M. Miller Communications
14415 Donnington Lane
Truckee CA 96161
www.rmmcartoons.com
email: info@robertmmiller.com

Cover Design by
Silver Moon Graphics
www.silvermoongraphics.com

Introduction

The only cartoons I know how to draw are veterinary and cowboy cartoons. I started cartooning while I was still in a high chair. Once I started school I cartooned mainly in order to pass them to my classmates so that the laughter would harass the teachers and liven up the dullness of the school day. Amazingly, throughout my schooling, including eight and a half years of college, I never got into trouble because of my daily cartooning. I guess cartooning must be the most benign way of lampooning other people.

Cowboying every summer, until I finally became a veterinarian at age thirty, provided a lot of cartoon ideas. During the summer of 1950, while working for a rancher in Sedalia, Colorado, my boss suggested selling my cartoons to the Western Horseman magazine. They were located in Colorado Springs, and although I couldn't believe anybody would actually pay me for my drawings, I was given a weekday off to visit the magazine. Editor (and later publisher), Dick Spencer, himself a successful cartoonist, bought all of the sketches I had with me. I have cartooned for that publication ever since. Encouraged by my success, I did cowboy cartoons for many other livestock, rodeo, and ranch magazines until I became a veterinarian in 1956.

In 1957, I moved to Thousand Oaks, California with my new bride. In 1959, I was struggling to make a living in a country practice; although the area was rich in animal population, it had never before had a practicing veterinarian. For extra income, I started to cartoon for the veterinary journals, but, I planned to stop drawing as soon as my practice was busy enough to warrant it. In fact, I cartooned for the journals as "RMM", hoping to remain anonymous. Previously, my cowboy cartoons were signed "Bob Miller." I felt that if my identity were known, it would obscure my identity as a veterinarian. I was right because, after a publisher revealed who RMM was without my permission, I became well-known within the veterinary profession primarily as a cartoonist.

Even today colleagues meet me at conventions and ask, "Where do you get your ideas? Have you ever practiced?" I tell them the truth. I practiced for 32 years and my work weeks generally ran from 65 to as much as 90 hours a week. Even during my last three years, when I had reduced my working days to four a week, I was still averaging 55 hours weekly. I never spent more than one hour a month cartooning until recently, when I retired from practice to take up a career in journalism and teaching.

It is very appropriate to combine cowboy and veterinary cartoons in a single volume. Cowboys and ranchers are all amateur veterinarians. Some of them are remarkably good at it. Others botch their cases, causing their patients more harm than good, but on the other hand, real veterinarians do that too, sometimes.

So the cowboys and ranchers are going to understand all the veterinary cartoons in this book. Veterinarians who do livestock and horse practice are going to understand the cowboy cartoons. A lot of veterinarians are also amateur cowboys. This is especially true in the western states, but it occurs in the rest of the nation as well, and I've certainly seen it in Canada. Many veterinarians enjoy the sport of rodeo, either on a professional basis, or as a hobby. There are a few veterinarians who are star contestants.

Many more veterinarians, myself included, view a day working a roundup or a branding as the ultimate form of recreation. To some that would seem to be a "busman's holiday", but the love of the outdoors and being around animals is what attracted us to the veterinary profession in the first place, so it's understandable. I can't think of anything I'd rather do than gather cattle in rugged Western terrain mounted on a good horse (although nowadays I mostly ride mules). Sometimes I wonder why so many of us love that kind of activity. I guess it satisfies mankind's instinct to hunt, without harming the prey. Too, there is a special joy in the harmony possible between horse and man. Then there's the clean air, the big sky, the open country. The people who read this book and understand the cartoons know what I mean. There's no way to explain it to the rest.

RMM
Bob Miller, D.V.M.
Thousand Oaks, California

THE ASSISTANT

"Here! You put this steel helmet on an' take the point!"

is may not be a profitable business, but one must consider
intangible benefits, such as the lifestyle one enjoys.

Doc, you think they're gittin' enough graze or should I be puttin' out some cake?

Ole Doc gets kinda pooped out after palpatin' a couple hunnert head, so we try to help 'im out.

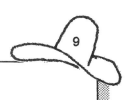

"Turning to the West, Tex and his faithful pony headed towards the glory of the setting sun."

♪ Mothers don't let your babies grow up to be cowboys..... ♫

♪ Goodbye Ole Paint.... ♪

"What kind of dogs did you say these are?"

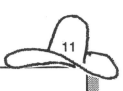

That's the bull calf you was ropin' an' throwin' an' tyin' all day long before you went off to college, son.

"So, what d'yd think of this filly, Doc?"

We brought our mare to breed to your stud.

Harley sure thinks alot of that Navajo blanket, don't he?

"Watch that badger hole," Tom!

For the first time, after packing into the high country for over thirty years, C.J. understood how a hobbled horse could move so far and so fast in a single night.

"The cowboy, always unwilling to dismount if it isn't absolutely necessary, becomes very adept at opening and closing ranch gates from horseback."

The legend of Poco Scissorhooves.

How long you been doing this?

It used to be that when a feller had to go you just used a stall, now there's nuthin' but wimmin aroun'.

GO FOR DOUGH
Fastest Horse in The West

Wow! What a slide!

Good thing we calve in April, any
earlier would be hard on them.

This one'll do! It's just a small wedding!

Whut in hell's got these horses
all buzzed up this morning'?

Say, doctor, you don't happen to have some of that DMSO, do you, for my old horse up at the cow camp? He's got a sore back.

I <u>tole</u> yew that mushroom cloud warn't no nuclear test! He burnt th' beef agin!

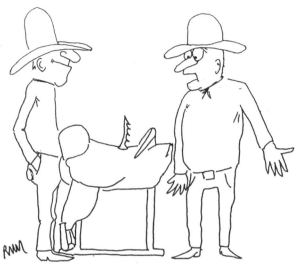

Well, aside from the fact that PRCA would never approve it, how would you get off?

Are you a registered guest?

I like Paints . . .
just so they don't have any white on them.

Yeah, we wuz in Denver fer the Stock
Show an' Betsy got me to a department
store an' I got trampled.

Well, with legs like hers, who'd want her?

I have reason to suspect that Clayton has been giving his doggin' horse large doses of steroids.

This will make a <u>great</u> poem for the Gathering at Elko!

Yew guys shore dress funny!

When it's Springtime in the Rockies . . . .

I called as soon as I seen she wuz lookin' poorly, Doc.

It was right after the Blackleg epidemic.
He follered me home one day.

Blessed is the shepherd that tendeth his flock!

Man, this is the best foal we ever raised. Put him in the pasture with the old dull barbed wire.

It's okay M'am! He's registered!

Phil's love of hunting was not so much inspired by his desire to kill, as it was by his need to escape the stridency of big city life and to savor the quiet and majesty of the forest.

That's one hell of a horse, Shorty,
but how do you mount him?

Hey, Coosie, sorry to hear about us losin' that mule yesterday!

It's not as bad as it looks, Bill. He'll be scarred, but in a few weeks he'll be back to work.

Did I show you my new pleasure horse bit?

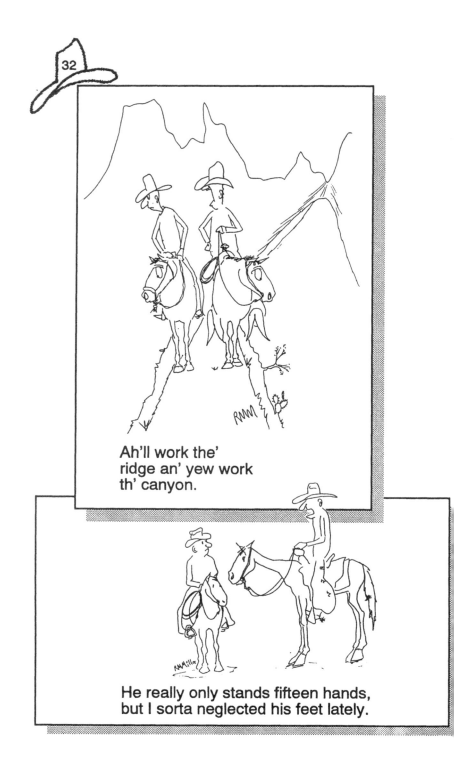

Ah'll work the'
ridge an' yew work
th' canyon.

He really only stands fifteen hands,
but I sorta neglected his feet lately.

The day 'ole Buck was forgiven for everything he'd ever done wrong.

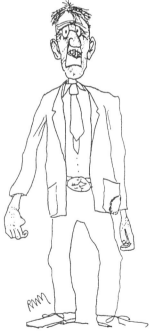

How'd yew know ah wuz a cowboy when ah'm all dressed up in city clothes?

It's my own idea . . .a saddlehorn that blows!

This, sir, is the toughest buckin'
horse in the country!

Jesse inhaled deeply, drinking in the fragrant sage-scented clean Western air.

<u>Flank 'im</u> down, Clyde! <u>Flank</u> 'im down!

Yeah, I know, but she gives us a good calf every year. Let's run her again.

So ah sez, "Hell yes, ah kin ride anything with hair on it!" an' he sez, "Well, okay, yer hired!"

Yep, the fingers is gone, but ah kep' the thumb. You gotta know whut yer doing'!

Is it too strong? Why hell, ah spilled some on Pete's boot awhile ago an' it broke his toe.

Gilbert is a veritable stallion!

"When yer ropin' in the brush, son, yew jus' got to plow on through!"

"Oh, hell, ah ain't prejudiced. Some of my best friends are city people!"

You left one behind, Carl!

It's not the horse, doctor! It's Simpson.
He's been on a crash diet to make the
weight, and I think he needs something.

The Dilemma - Whether to walk back to
headquarters after being dumped, or to
give Sancho ten dollars for his burro.

Are you the MacPherson who invented the
MacPherson bullfighting costume?

Okay Baldwin, I warned you
once before! You're fired!

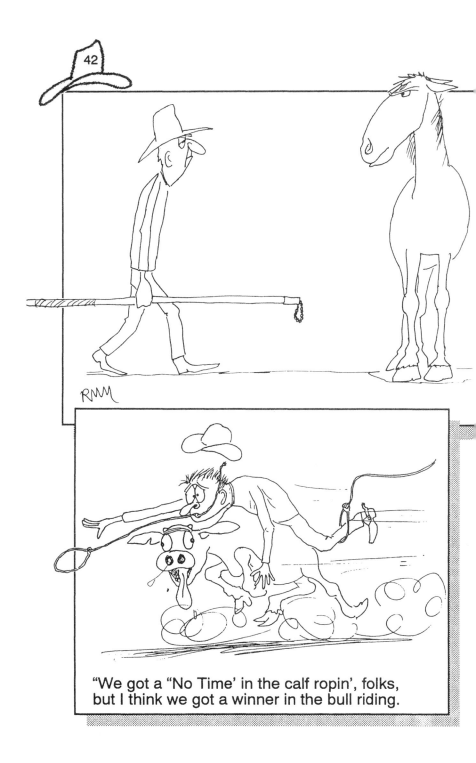

"We got a "No Time' in the calf ropin', folks, but I think we got a winner in the bull riding.

"Mounted Police, M'am!"

Granted the sperm count is low, but
look at the size of the little devils!

The trouble is, by the time they get out to where the feed is, they're dehydrated again an' need to come in for water.

"But if we roll her on her back to slide her off, her horns will go down in the cattle guard."

Be real quiet...as long as you can hear hoofbeats and spurs jinglin'. When that stops and you hear them swearin' at the thorns, we break and run.

ugust: You guys are lucky up here in
lberta. Why down where ah come
om we got thorns an' we got turrible
eat, an' we got chiggers, an' we got. . .

6 Months Later:

Towards the end of the Twentieth Century . . . .
Larry busts an axle in the Northwest lava rock
section and uses his cellular phone to send an
angry FAX message to the pickup manufacturer
in Tokyo.

Oh no! Not again! <u>BEHIND</u> the hump,
Eriksson! <u>BEHIND</u> the hump!

My neighbor, Johnson, asked me to tell you to drop by while you're out this way, Doc. He's got some work for you an' he's just up the road a piece.

"Oh, oh! Watch it folks! That last bull jumped the arena fence and he's out there on the fairgrounds....and there go the pick up men after the loose bull.

Your saddlebag's open, Ma'm . . . . .
Holy mackeral!

Just remember, yer not in South Dakota now.
Yew don't dare git bucked off!

Calvin nearly died laughing last night, before they turned in, when he heard about how Spencer had freaked out at finding a snake in his boot.

Amazing how much better spaghetti tastes the second day than it does the first, an' even better the third day, an' even better the fourth day, an' . .

Have you heard about the new, no-rotation, once-in-a-lifetime paste wormer?

My backaches have disappeared since I started riding but my horse has to take Butazolidin.

I didn't say "better" road, Doc, I said "shorter!"

I did recommend a garden hose to relieve bloat, but I meant a short piece, to allow the gas to escape.

Look Cindy, the wrangler! I didn't recognize him without his hat and chaps.

I never give a thought to gettin' bucked off— as a kid the rocks and cactus were so thick 'round home, I didn't dare get bucked off. . .

Man, I can hardly wait to see this foal!

Well, Doc, she hasn't paid her way for the last three years, but, by wife says I don't either— so let's run her one more year.

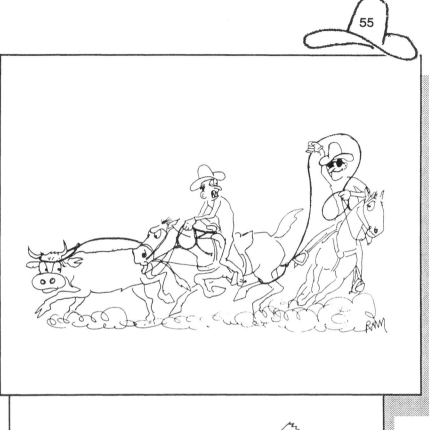

Where's my steer?

We call it Miraclemycin!

News Item: Humane groups campaign against raising veal calves in confinement; maintain they have right to be free out in the open.

I sympathize with your viewpoint but, you see, it's a tradition in my family to eat meat. We've been doing it for two million years.

Hey! Was that lubricant or soap I put on this tube?

Well, we don't do any vaccinating on our place, and <u>none</u> of the survivors ever get sick!

Boy, I was proud of my King Cobra boots, but Chimpanzee?

Yer doin' fine, son. A couple more rides and you'll be ready to solo.

Hey! you're making the mud all dirty!

My hat! My new hat!

What do you know about hemorrhoids, Doc?

He's afraid of men.

We just bought him for Karen. The man said he's a great kid's horse, but we thought we'd have you look at him before we got too attached!

Oh, I don't dare feed him grain. He'll get too frisky!

Rain's startin' to soak through my bedroll, Al!

There she is, Doc, with her old
prolapse ahangin' out of 'er!

A cowboy who often bucked off
got purty sick of it (cough)
After sev'ral bad times,
I can't think of what rhymes,
so I guess I'll just up an' quit (cough).

Reride! Reride!

————Okay, Ron! We got him cut and branded and ear-marked and as soon as I get back on my horse you can turn loose of his head.

Okay men, there's a low pressure system moving in, the barometer is falling, the humidity rising, and the prevailing wind from the Northeast. Let's start the Rain Dance.

I fenced the whole place, because I came into some money. I didn't pay my vet bill.

You mean you've never played cholla?

We had her palpated at 35 days and she was pregnant. That was 13 months ago and we're getting worried.

You could write a book, Doc!
You could call it "All critters, big an' little!"

This is the first time I've seen the owner get a nosebleed!

The grooming and bathing area at a horse show is a beehive of activity . . . . a beauty parlor for horses.

Wait, Doctor. I don't want you to go in there without me. He's a mean S.O.B.!

It's OK, I've got everything under control!

Next to his saddle, a cowboy's most treasured posession is his boots.

I can't give you a diagnosis. Will you settle for a prognosis?

Don't worry about the side effects, Doc. It's the rear effects you need to watch out for.

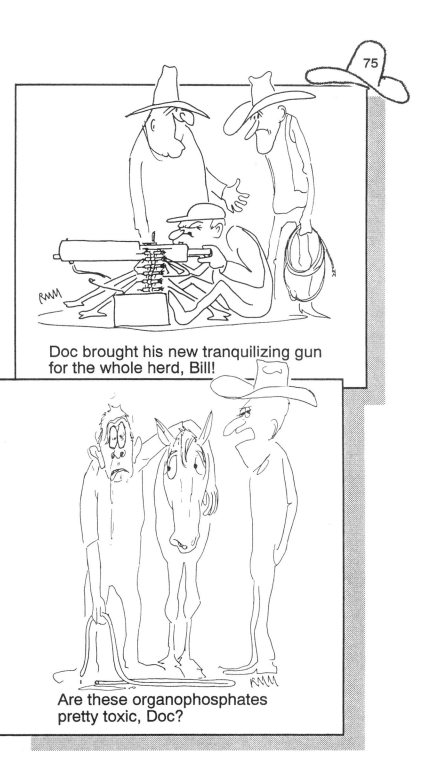

Doc brought his new tranquilizing gun for the whole herd, Bill!

Are these organophosphates pretty toxic, Doc?

Gad, what a gopher!

You say that using a colicky horse to pull you out of the mud may actually help his colic?

Why can't you turn back horseback, like everyone else?

Wait, Doc, wait! My cow's still in your chute!

How fortunate you are to be able to spend your life caring for God's little creatures.

THE BEEPER

The Yank's a good bloke. Maybe we ought to tell him that they aren't really calves.

I didn't hear you drive up, Doc.

Howdy, Doctor Reinow.
Say, you know that "kill or cure" stuff you gave
 the bull?. . . You were right.

My saddle! My new saddle!

I don't know what she has, but it's the worst case of it I've ever seen!

Why Skeeter, I didn' know you could yodel!
That's right purty!

This is the Polled Texas Longhorn—
the breed of the future!

He's in lousy shape!

That ain't the brandin' you smell, sir. It's the roper's hand. This is dally country you know.

I got manure on my new ostrich boots!

Let me know if it needs more chili.

You wanted the other veterinarian?
I _am_ the other veterinarian—
I haven't been to bed for four nights!

Grandson, until a century ago the Indians survived in this country off of the buffalo. Now we're tryin' to do the same thing with cattle. Of course, the government screwed up the Indians' way of life, an' now they're tryin' to do the same thing to us.

Doctor Hasenretcher is out to lunch.
May I take a message?

You're supposed to be here for physical therapy Mister Davenport, not to practice your bronc riding on our examination tables!

Ride's over, cowboy. . . hey, Buddy, the whistle blew. . . you can quit now!

I can't understand it. I even gave her cortisone.

I've decided that we ought to sell the ranch, Dorthy. I'm sick and tired of the weather, the hard work, and the risk.

Doc, the old cow's in trouble. How much is a call?

You'll have to excuse my husband. He's a broodmare specialist and it takes him a few days to realize he's on vacation.

CUTTING COMPETITION
SAT-SUN - JUNE 3-4
$1500 PURSE

I guess I misunderstood the sign.

Yes, he's twenty hands. . .
if you count his ears!

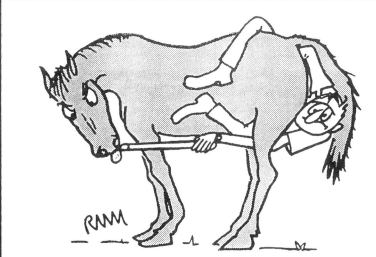

How to palpate for pregnancy without getting kicked.

Wilbur, why don't you let someone else handle the iron for a while?

Do we take him to a doctor or a dentist?

I been waitin' here for a vet truck to pass.
I need some teeth floated.

No! Not that one, doctor!
It's this one I'm worried about.

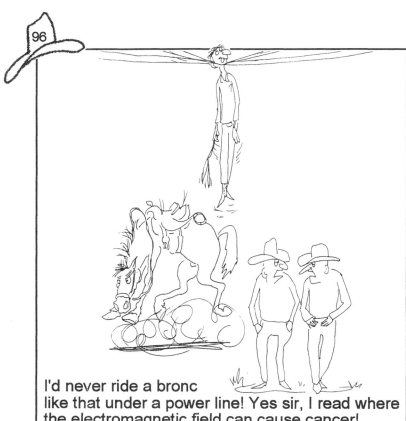

I'd never ride a bronc
like that under a power line! Yes sir, I read where
the electromagnetic field can cause cancer!

How lucky you are to be able to do your work
so close to the earth.

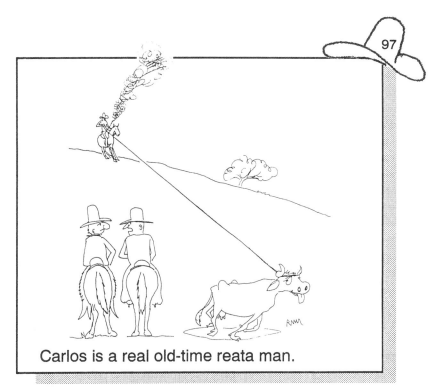

Carlos is a real old-time reata man.

You brought in the wrong heifer?
Just when everything was going great!
You've ruined my day!

Say, you talk about horns! I'll show you a set o' horns!

So, you're Doctor Purcell, who takes care of my daughter's horse! I'd shake hands, ordinarily.

Cold, dear?

Aw! It's a long way from his heart, Doc, but he's a good pony an' I figgered to let the vet take a look at him.

Why you can't beat Western Colorado.
Al, tell the truth! Did you ever see a
view like this in Nebraska?

I don't see Prince in his corral. Didn't he make it
after I treated him last week?

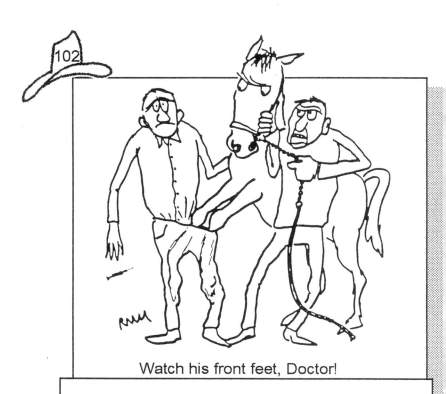

Watch his front feet, Doctor!

Yer s'posed to use th' catalogs!
The *Western Horseman*'s there to read!

Yes, Santa was good to me.
I had only one call Christmas Eve.

Mine's a mule too, but his ears froze off last winter!

Good news, Ed! It's not laminitis.
He's just frozen to the ground!

I thought YOU were hazing!

Bubba's blockin' his hat again over th' coffee pot. It'll be a while!

"Pick-up and delivery truck" doesn't mean they are designed for obstetrics! You're not supposed to pull calves with a pickup!

I don't care how many trophy buckles you've won— you're still disqualified.

Yes, I'm Doctor Kill-the-bull-quickly. But, let's not be formal. Please just call me Kill-the-bull.

Hey look, Slim. . . A pair of eagles soarin' aroun' down there!

Now there'd be a money ride if he was spurrin' a little harder.

Ole Buck's only twelve but, you know, this country is hard on a pony's legs.

Hold everything! . . some wise guy put chili pepper on his piggin' string.

I wonder where George went with that hotshot?

Maybe we'd win one of these wild cow milkin' contests some day if you'd learn to milk by hand!

Get up mules! Hup, Daisy!, Hup, Red!, Hup Jasper! Hup! Hup!

What? You **ate** my patient?

You'll need your rubber boots, Doc.

Are you a good guy or a bad guy?

Well, that's the spring branding this year. See you when we gather in the fall. . . about 5 weeks.

What do you mean, 'Grass Founder'?

Yes, yes, she's in estrus. . .
now move her forward, for gosh sakes!

What's Quiche?

Now, here's a really modern boot. . . low walking heel, extra low tops, laced for easy on and off, composition sole, and economical too.

I think I felt a foal.
Why don't we run a blood test to be sure?

No, I'm going to do this one standing. Frankly, I
have trouble bending down this soon after lunch!

I thought <u>you</u> were the pickup man!

Abu Bey has been that way ever since he subscribed to *The Western Horseman*.

I _told_ you not to feed out of a barrel at home!

Someday these millions and millions of buffalo will be gone,
and they will be replaced by the white man's sheep and cattle,
and their belching will produce methane which will cause
global warming.

Outside! Outside!

Waldo Claghorn! Drybone, New Mexico!

This may not be a profitable business, but one must consider the intangible benefits, such as the lifestyle one enjoys.

Wait 'til you see what we found during the spring thaw!

Acknowledgements

Many of the cartoons in this book are new and have never been published under any other title. Others have previously appeared in a variety of veterinary journals, horse and livestock magazines, and trade publications. My thanks to all those who gave me permission to reprint those previously published cartoons: Western Horseman, Modern Veterinary Practice, the California Veterinarian, Veterinary Medicine, American Veterinary Publications, The Messanger, The E. E. Massengill Co, and Veterinary Forum.

Published by Robert M. Miller Communications
Truckee, CA
Visit us at www.RobertMmiller.com

Other Works by Dr. Robert M. Miller

Books

Natural Horsemanship Explained - From Heart to Hands
The Revolution in Horsemanship - Co-authored with Rick Lamb
Understanding the Ancient Secrets of the Horse's Mind
Imprint Training of the Newborn Foal
Yes, We Treat Aardvarks
Mind Over Miller
Handling the Equine Patient - A Manual for Veterinary Students & Technicians

Equine Videos

Understanding Horses
Safer Horsemanship
Early Learning
Control of the Horse
Influencing the Horse's Mind
The Causes of Lameness

Cartoon Books

Am I Getting To Old For This?
The Second Oldest Profession
A Midstream Collection

Websites

www.robertmmiller.com
www.rmmcartoons.com
www.thepassionforhorses.com

Printed in the USA
CPSIA information can be obtained
at www.ICGtesting.com
LVHW020310061224
798476LV00008B/268

* 9 7 8 0 9 8 4 4 6 2 0 3 2 *